FINISHING LINE PRESS

www.finishinglinepress.com

Intrastate Lines

poems and artwork by

Alexandra "Zan" Delaine Hailey

Finishing Line Press
Georgetown, Kentucky

Intrastate Lines

ACKNOWLEDGMENT

Poem 16. was previously published in *Circling With Poets Laureate: Prince
William Poet Laureate Circle and Invited Laureates: A Poetry Anthology.*
Edited by James P. Wagner. Long Island, NY: Local Gems Press, September
18, 2023.

This chapbook was made possible in part by donations to the ONE LAST
WORD Program. ONE LAST WORD helps to bring the last works of gifted
poets to the world.

Publisher: Leah Huete de Maines
Editor: Christen Kincaid
Cover Art: Alexandra "Zan" Delaine Hailey
Author Photo: Alexandra "Zan" Delaine Hailey
Cover Design: The Hailey Family & Elizabeth Maines McCleavy

Order online: www.finishinglinepress.com
also available on amazon.com

Author inquiries and mail orders:
Finishing Line Press
PO Box 1626
Georgetown, Kentucky 40324
USA

For all the wanderers.

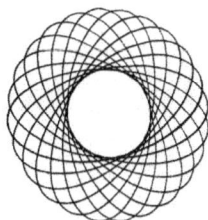

1.

Like May Hibiscus,
dunes stretch,
beating peach cream
blues in harmony
with a golden plasmic
tempo, rise tonal shadows
in complementary velocitic
degrees, gaining height
above northern deciduous,
force me to put on
my sunglasses before
hiding behind a shield
of perfect tea grey.

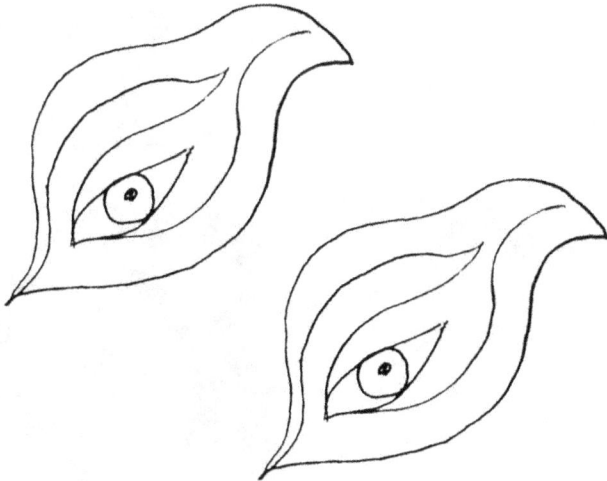

2.

Mud,
like time,
seeps between
my fingers
as I stand—
rocks embedded
in my knees.

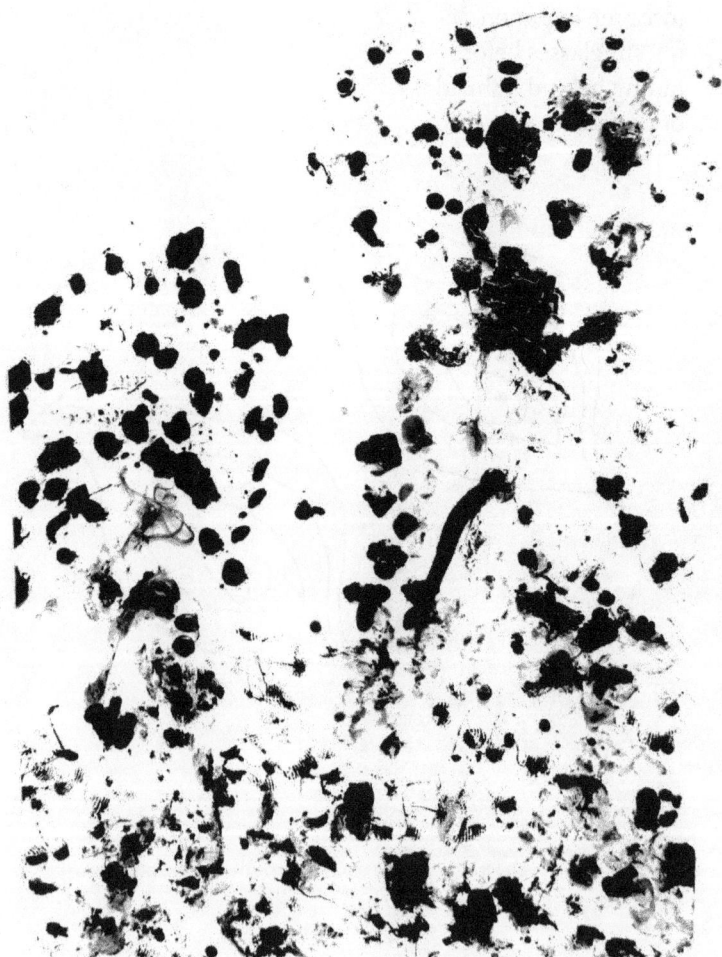

3.

It's another fuchsia-sun day.
but this time I only catch
a glimpse as the setting sky
disappears behind the sound
barriers that line this Delmarva
strip of I-95 between Baltimore
and Silver Spring, like the summer
canopy behind fog, driving me west
in the golden hour rush,
before disappearing as the motorway
forks toward the cardinal state,
relaying a simple July formula
for hypothetical dreamers
that fish from the moon
without bait for the stars.

4.

I am from the back roads
between here there and everywhere
because the Beatles will forever hold
number one. Even 12th Planet notes
A Day in the Life as the greatest song.

5.

I scale the stars
with smoke clouds,
my feet slipping
into the toes
of my shoes
each toe bending
more and more
at the knuckle,
as they meet
the interior,
heat squeezes
my brain waves
sending thermal
shocks through
my psyche.

6.

The bumble bee is such a brute
for a nectar lover,
unlike butterflies who ride
nectar palettes like west
coast waves, drawing nectar
in the breeze.

7.

Irises: Saint Remy, May 1890

Prussian blue petals wave
and reach, ranging
in hues to *pure*
carmine, whose
verdant stacks
disappear
like a thunderstorm
into the wet
depths of golden vases
that stand against
a gleaming room
walled in striking
lemon yellow.

8.

Dream against starstruck currents.
The moon awaits your embrace.

9.

Vincent VanGogh to Theo, Arles 1888

Bear in mind
no mortal
poisonous
zinc white
without mercy
to paint them
a Garden of Olives—
red earth,
crimson trunks,
sky: lemon yellow—
faces the blade.
Orchards again.

10.

Four short days
can change the world
and each unattended
Feng Shui dream
is just another moment
lost in a handshake.

11.

At West Shore and Beechwood
not a single Beech tree
fertilizes flourishing branches
of dainty nuts, but the Pileated
Woodpecker laughs in hysterics
from the tipped top
of the crab apple tree
as lily pads tread by the shore
of its shadow. And I smile
thinking, this will be the day—
Big orange ball, sinking
in the water, sweet breeze
kissing my bare feet.

12.

Beneath rattling planked
ways that line
from semi to stage,
we sit like troll people
out of the wet—
for clouds can cry, even
when just this morning
they were so close
you could taste them.

13.

Tomorrow winds westward,
north through the valleys,
leaves shifting
to the color wheel's
warmer side of deciduous,
while you await
justice's upcoming vote
behind barrier gates
that separate the "sick"
from society.

14.

Velvet orange meringue
slips across tips
of conifers, like Corduroy
Bear's English muffin,
dribble gliding
beneath the cumulonimbus
folds of his handkerchief—
washed away
with cratered glows,
lurking the horizon,
as twilight catches
a glimpse of the golden
hour, Ra whispers,
Color me ripe
nectarine.

15.

I work six days a week—
Sunday through Friday—
Saturday is a day
of a differing flow,
a day of hellos
and goodbyes. Saturday
is not a workday.
But today is Saturday,
and today I am working.

16.

I hope you see the sun rise
and I hope you look right
into its climbing fire
because there's a chunk
of morning when that's more
than okay.

I hope you take advantage of the moment—

stop to sit on the fence and watch
houses paint watercolor portraits
across the pond's surface
and I hope you always catch
a glimpse of the cattails blooming
like white linen in autumn—

when the moment presents itself.

17.

Desolate parks
line 206 from base
to the ocean
      periodically
          spaced
              out
between seemingly endless rows
of Holly red and burnt sienna bushes,
driving warm hues at the wintering
feet of slightly cyaned-grey
sky with curls that roll horizontal
like the four fathers once wigged,
behind a mighty pen,
a John Hancock
and an incandescent
blueprint.

19.

Forever on ice,
sinking figure eights
into frozen satin,
grading flakes
in a beveling trail.

20.

Then there's this point
when the face of a stranger
is all too familiar and even
though the cities change,
the faces seem
to stay the same.

Darling, follow me
into the next dimension
where the face I recognize
is the only one I know,
from skin to bone
and back out the skull,

while sitting at another false
marble bar in another
hotel lounge—past the revolving
door and well-lit champagne
lobby, where cigarette smoke
rarely drifts past the first

fanned notch. Although each
moment is sonified
by an unforgettable laugh,
the resonance simply slips
into words served with
tomorrow's corrective breakfast.

Afterword

Notes

Poem 4. alludes to "Here, There, and Everywhere," the Beatles song her parents chose for their first dance at their wedding. "A Day in the Life," is a Beatles song she loved, and she adapted its title for a memoir she wrote in college.

In Poem 7. "Irises: Saint Remy, May 1890," the italicized color phrases, *Prussian blue* and *pure carmine*, appear in Vincent van Gogh's Letter 870 To Theo van Gogh. Saint-Rémy-de-Provence, Sunday, 11 May 1890. The full letter is available through the Van Gogh Museum at https://vangoghletters. org/vg/letters/let870/letter.html.

In Poem 9. "Vincent van Gogh to Theo, Arles 1888," most of the words and phrases in the poem appear scattered in Letter 637 To Theo van Gogh. Arles, Sunday, 8 or Monday, 9 July 1888. The full letter is available through the Van Gogh Museum at https://www.vangoghletters.org/vg/letters/let637/letter. html#translation.

Poem 11. includes the line, "Big orange ball, sinking in the water," the first line of Kenny Chesney's song, "How Forever Feels," Track 2 on the album, *Everywhere We Go*. Most lyric websites use the contraction sinkin' rather than sinking.

The Making of *Intrastate Lines*

Alexandra completed this series of poems arranged as a chapbook manuscript as early as 2015. The poems, originally referred to as "Highway Poetry," later collected as *Intrastate Lines*, were never individually titled—instead numbered 1-20—and mysteriously never included a #18. We are grateful to Leah Maines, editor at Finishing Line Press, for selecting *Intrastate Lines* for publication through the One Last Word program, and to Christen Kincaid, editor. Unfortunately, we lost Alexandra in a tragic car accident in 2018 while she was working in Paducah, Kentucky. She was 26 years old.

Alexandra's poetry and art fill journals, sketchbooks, and canvases, all contributing to keeping her spirit alive, her creativity inspiring all who love her to create ourselves. The poems she curated as a manuscript for *Intrastate Lines* are now accompanied by art—her ink and pencil drawings—we selected, not to be illustrative but to complement her poems. Though the poems and drawings stand alone, we hope they also enhance each other. Alexandra rarely wrote a single page without a doodle in the margin. Although she left us five and a half years ago, we are comforted that her words and art will continue to flourish.

As Poet Laureate of Prince William County, Alexandra facilitated local writing workshops in which she incorporated ekphrasis—both from writing to visual art and from visual art to writing—along with oral readings of Vincent van Gogh's letters to his brother Theo. She would collect words and phrases from a letter and encourage the audience to do the same. Those words and phrases might inspire writing or art in any form. She named the project "Ekphrasticize That!" and later took it on the road to the Northern Virginia Writing Project at George Mason University and the Psychology Department at Virginia Commonwealth University.

In honor of Alexandra's Poet Laureate project and the way she was inspired by artists and creators across the disciplines, proceeds from sales of *Intrastate Lines* will help fund prizes for a new category in The Poetry Society of Virginia's Annual Contest due on Edgar Allan Poe's Birthday, January 19th:

Category 22. ALEXANDRA "ZAN" DELAINE HAILEY MEMORIAL. Inspired by an artist or a creator across the disciplines. Awards: $50, $30, $20. Sponsored by the Hailey family.

Submission details can be found on the website of The Poetry Society of Virginia: poetrysocietyofvirginia.org. We encourage you to submit a poem.

Gratitude

On behalf of Alexandra "Zan" Delaine Hailey, the Hailey family would like to thank all the relatives, friends, educators, artists, and creators across the disciplines who inspired her to be successful in all she did. We are grateful to Kathy Smaltz, Natalie Potell, and Alice Mergler for writing blurbs and for reading Alexandra's poems on our Zan Zoom celebration of *Intrastate Lines* along with Michelle Garcia, Neil Hailey, and Cathy Hailey. You can view the recording on YouTube: https://www.youtube.com/watch?v=av4ZJba3RIY.

Many communities contributed to Alexandra's ability to thrive as a person and as an artist:

◊ Alexandra's extended family and friends
◊ Virginia Commonwealth University educators and students
◊ Woodbridge Senior High School Center for the Fine and Performing Arts, Advanced Placement Program, and *Eddas* Literary/Arts Magazine communities of educators, coaches, and students
◊ Early educators at Lake Ridge Middle School, Parkside Middle School, Old Bridge Elementary School, Mockingbird Preschool, and Miss Diane's Daycare
◊ The Greek American and Eastern Orthodox communities
◊ Occoquan Forest neighborhood
◊ The Northern Virginia Writing Project at George Mason University, including the Student Summer Institute and Saturday Young Writers Workshops
◊ The Prince William Poet Laureate Program and Poet Laureate Circle
◊ The extended Poet Laureate community of invitees and guests at In the Company of Laureates, especially in 2015 and 2017
◊ Write by the Rails and Virginia Writers Club
◊ Virginia Festival of the Book and Fall for the Book
◊ The daVinci Center and entrepreneurship community at VCU and in the City of Richmond
◊ The Poetry Society of Virginia
◊ Spotlight Dance LLC (tap, jazz, ballet, pointe, hip hop)
◊ The diverse music scenes in RVA, NOVA, and beyond
◊ Vans and MASS skateboarding communities
◊ The natural world

We appreciate all of you!
　　　　　　　—Cathy, Ken, and Neil Hailey

From an early age, **Alexandra "Zan" Delaine Hailey** (1992-2018) had a passion for writing, art, dance, and music as both a practitioner and a consumer. She lived as an artist, experimenting with all genres of writing and all forms of visual arts: painting, drawing, photography, sculpture, and furniture making, among other arts and crafts. She was constantly working towards inventing new products and processes, and she loved to research and learn whatever it took to understand new concepts. Alexandra served as an inaugural poet laureate in Prince William County, VA, 2014-2016. Her poet laureate project, "Ekphrasticize That!" focused on ekphrastic writing and art along with inspiration from the letters of Vincent van Gogh to his brother Theo. Alexandra studied English and Creative Writing at Virginia Commonwealth University, where Gary Sange, Gregory Donovan, and David Wojahn helped her hone her poetry. Her writing has been published in *The Northern Virginia Review, A Wreath of Golden Laurels: An Anthology of Poetry by 100 Poets Laureate, Written in Arlington, The Poetry Society of Virginia Centennial Anthology, Circling With Poets Laureate, New Departures: Write by the Rails Anthology,* and Virginia Commonwealth University's Focused Inquiry Textbook. Alexandra died in a car accident in 2018 while she was working in Paducah, Kentucky. She was 26 years old.